All-American Gospel

The Best Collection of Gospel Music Ever Assembled!
Complete Vocal/Piano Sheet Music Arrangements

Arranged by Michael Johnson

HAL•LEONARD®
CORPORATION

7777 W. BLUEMOUND RD. P.O. BOX 13819 MILWAUKEE, WI 53213

Catalog #07-1105

ISBN# 1-56922-108-1

©1996 CREATIVE CONCEPTS PUBLISHING CORPORATION
Printed in the United States of America
All Rights Reserved

Produced by John L. Haag

Exclusive Distributor:
CREATIVE CONCEPTS PUBLISHING CORPORATION
6020-B Nicolle Street, Ventura, California 93003
Check out our Web site at *http://www.creativeconcepts.com* or you can Email us at *mail@creativeconcepts.com*

All-American Gospel

CONTENTS

Do, Lord

All God's Children Got Shoes

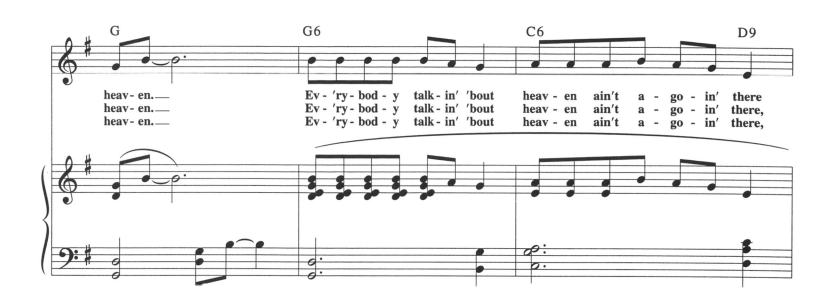

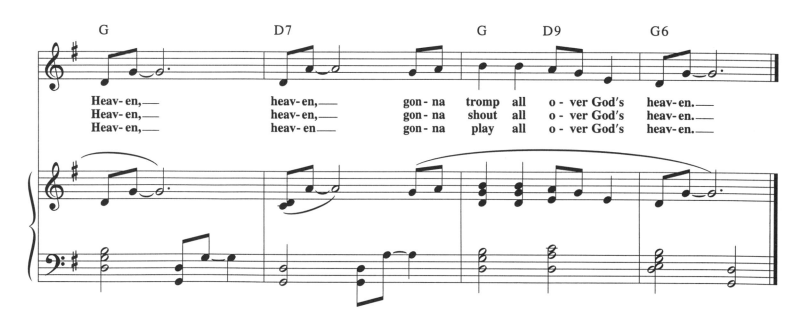

4.
I got a song, you got a song,
All God's children got songs.
When I get to heaven gonna sing my song,
Gonna sing all over God's heaven heaven, heaven
Ev'rybody talkin' 'bout heaven ain't a-goin' there,
Heaven, Heaven,
Gonna sing all over God's heaven

5.
I got wings, you got wings,
All God's children got wings.
When I get to heaven gonna put on my wings,
Gonna fly
All over God's heaven, heaven, heaven.
Ev'rybody talkin' 'bout heaven ain't a-goin' there,
Heaven, Heaven,
Gonna fly all over God's heaven

Amazing Grace

Words by John Newton
and John P. Rees

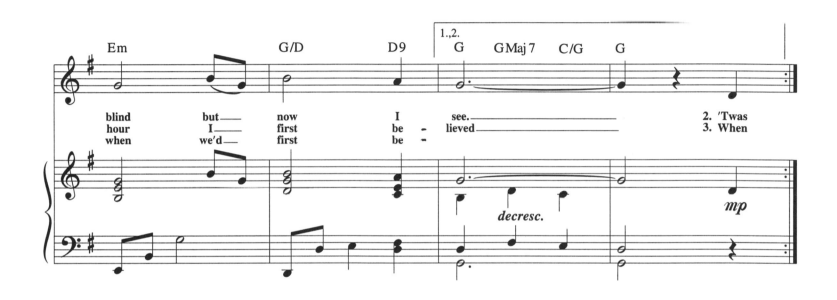

An Evening Prayer

Words & Music by
C.M. Battersby and
Charles H. Gabriel

1. If I have wound-ed an-y soul to-day, If I have caused one foot to go a-stray, If I have walked in my own will - ful way, Dear
2. If I have ut-tered i-dle word or vain, If I have turned a-side from want or pain, Lest I of-fend some oth-er thru the strain, Dear
3. If I have been per-verse or hard, or cold, If I have longed for shel-ter in Thy fold, When Thou has giv-en me some fort to hold, Dear

Blessed Assurance

Words by Fanny J. Crosby
Music by Phoebe P. Knapp

Brighten the Corner
Where You Are

Words by Ina Duley Ogden
Music by Charles H. Gabriel

15

By an' By

Deep River

Down by the Riverside

E♭
riv - er - side. Gon - na lay down my bur - den,
lay down my sword and shield
put on my long white robe
meet my loving Sav - ior
E♭ Gm7/D Cm
Down by the riv - er - side to
Fm E♭/B♭ B♭7 E♭ A♭/E♭
stu - dy war no more.
Chorus
E♭ Fm7 A♭
I ain't gon - na stu - dy war no more, I ain't gon - na

Doxology (Praise God)

Ev'ry Time I Feel the Spirit

27

Ezekiel Saw The Wheel

4. There's one thing sure that you can't do, 'way in the middle of the air,
   You can't serve God and Satan, too, 'way in the middle of the air.

   Chorus

5. One of these days about twelve o'clock, 'way in the middle of the air,
   This old world's gonna reel and rock, 'way in the middle of the air.

   Chorus

Give Me That Old Time Religion

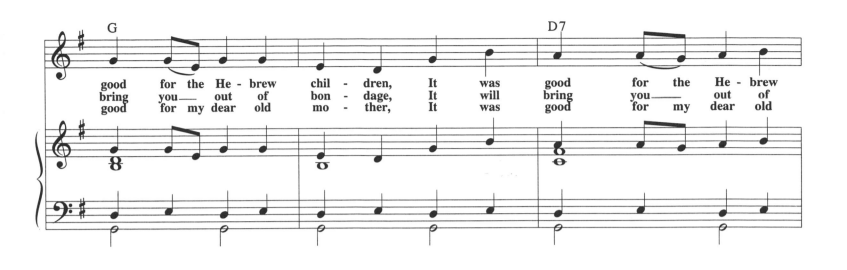

good for the He - brew chil - dren, It was good for the He - brew
bring you__ out of bon - dage, It will good bring you__ out of
good for my dear old mo - ther, It was good for my dear old

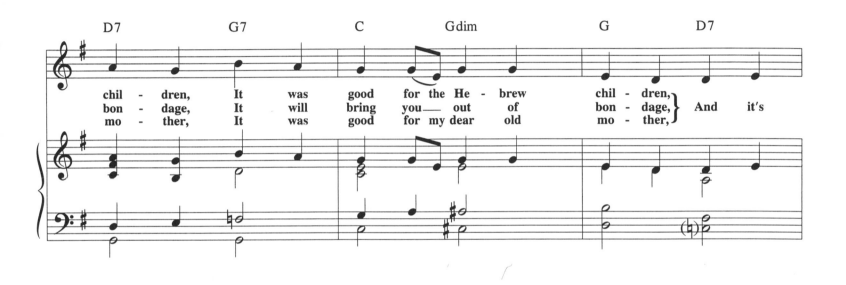

chil - dren, It was good for the He - brew chil - dren,
bon - dage, It will bring you__ out of bon - dage, } And it's
mo - ther, It was good for my dear old mo - ther,

good e - nough for me. Give Me That me.

Go Down, Moses

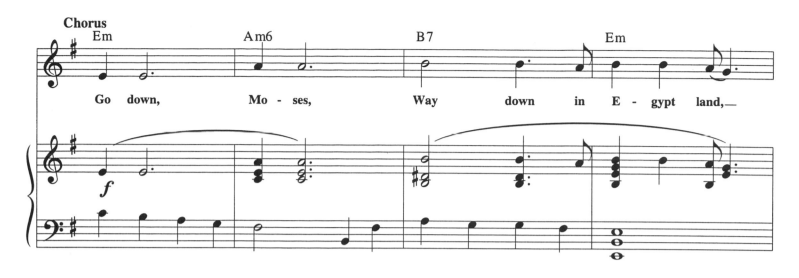

4.

Tle Lord told Moses what to do
Let my people go,
To lead the Hebrew children through
Let my people go.
Chorus

5.

O come along Moses, you won't get lost
Let my people go,
Stretch out your rod and come across,
Let my people go.
Chorus

6.

As Israel stood by the waterside,
Let my people go,
At God's command it did divide,
Let my people go.
Chorus

7.

When they reached the other shore
Let my people go,
They sang a song of triumph o'er,
Let my people go.
Chorus

8.

Pharoah said he'd go across,
Let my people go,
But Pharoah and his host were lost,
Let my people go.
Chorus

9.

Jordan shall stand up like a wall,
Let my people go,
And the walls of Jericho shall fall,
Let my people go.
Chorus

10.

Your foes shall not before you stand,
Let my people go,
And you'll possess fair Canaan's Land
Let my people go.
Chorus

11.

We need not always weep and mourn,
Let my people go,
And wear these slavery chains forlorn,
Let my people go.
Chorus

Good News

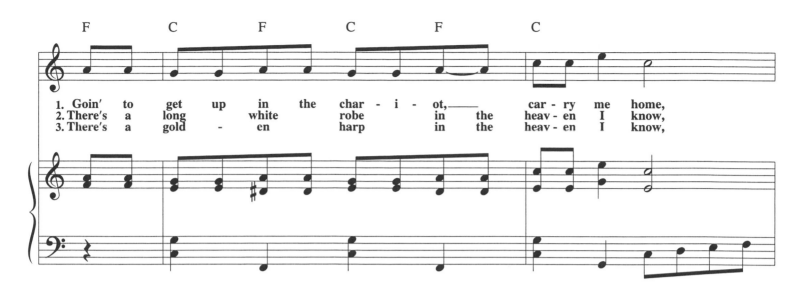

He's Got The Whole World
In His Hands

Hush! Hush!

I Need Thee Every Hour

Words by Annie S. Hawks
and Robert Lowry

Music by Robert Lowry

In the Garden

Words and Music by
C. Austin Miles

It Is Well With My Soul

Words by Horatio G. Spafford
Music by Philip P. Bliss

Jesus Loves Me

Words by Anna B. Warner
Music by William B. Bradbury

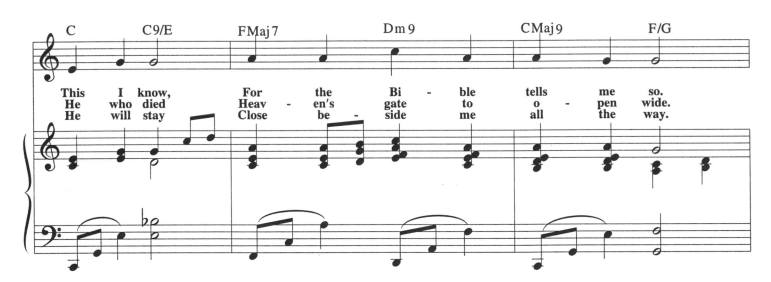

47

Joshua Fought the Battle of Jericho

You   may   talk a - bout your kings of   Gid - e - on,   You may
Well, the   Lord__ done__   told old   Josh - u - a,   "You must
Up__   to the walls of   Jer - i - cho   He__

talk a - bout your men of   Saul,   But there's none like good old
do__   just__ what I   say,ν March 'round that cit - y
marched__ with__ spear in   hand,   "Go__ blow those ram horns,"

Josh - u - a   At the bat - tle of Jer - i - cho. That morn - ing__
sev - en times, And the walls__ will tum - ble a - way." That morn - ing__
Josh - ua cried, "'Cause the bat - tle is in my__ hands." That morn - ing__

D.C. al fine

Just A Closer Walk With Thee

Just a clos - er walk with Thee.

Grant it, Je - sus, is my plea.

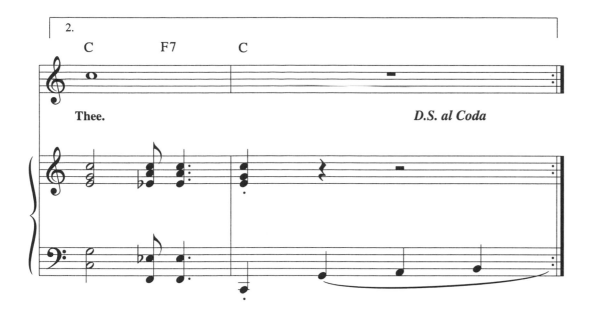

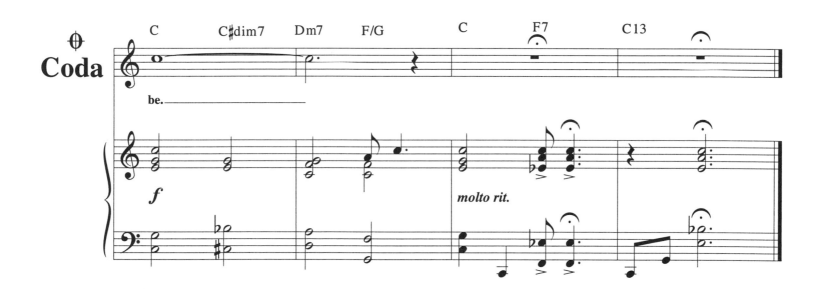

Just a Little Talk with Jesus

55

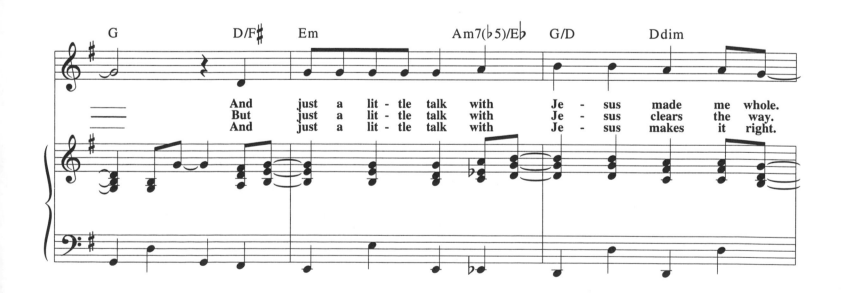

Just As I Am

Words by Charlotte Elliott
Music by William B. Bradbury

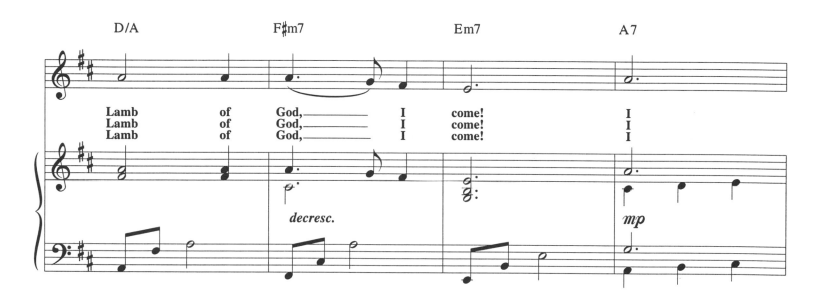

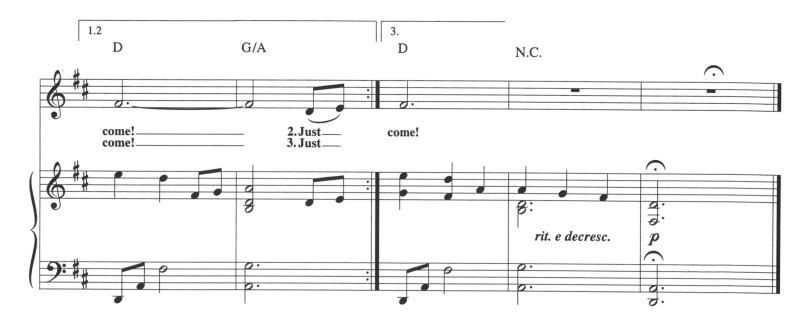

Get On Board

Kum Ba Yah

Slowly

1. Kum ba yah, my Lord, kum ba yah, Kum ba
2. Some-one's cry - ing, Lord, kum ba yah, Some-one's
3. Some-one's sing - ing, Lord, kum ba yah, Some-one's

yah, my Lord, kum ba yah! Kum ba yah, my Lord, kum ba
cry - ing, Lord, kum ba yah! Some-one's cry - ing, Lord, kum ba
sing - ing, Lord, kum ba yah! Some-one's sing - ing, Lord, kum ba

yah, O Lord, kum ba yah.
yah, O Lord, kum ba yah.
yah, O Lord, kum ba yah.

4. Someone's hoping, Lord, kum ba yah,
   Someone's hoping, Lord, kum ba yah!
   Someone's hoping, Lord, kum ba yah,
   O Lord, kum ba yah.

5. Someone's dancing, Lord, kum ba yah,
   Someone's dancing, Lord, kum ba yah!
   Someone's dancing, Lord, kum ba yah,
   O Lord, kum ba yah.

6. Someone's shouting, Lord, kum ba yah,
   Someone's shouting, Lord, kum ba yah!
   Someone's shouting, Lord, kum ba yah,
   O Lord, kum ba yah.

7. Someone's praying, Lord, kum ba yah,
   Someone's praying, Lord, kum ba yah!
   Someone's praying, Lord, kum ba yah,
   O Lord, kum ba yah.

The Lord's Prayer

by Felix Mendelssohn

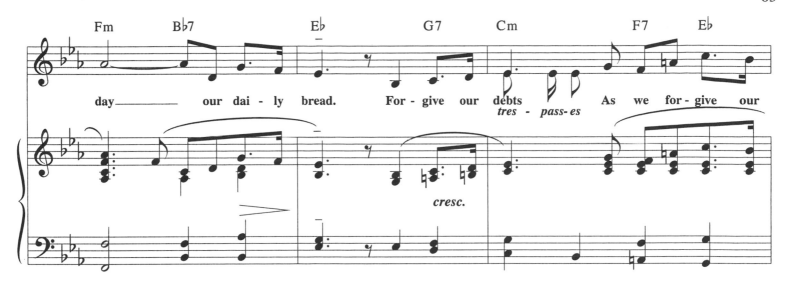

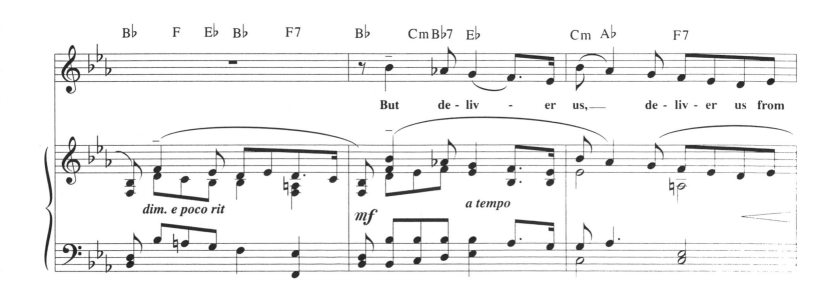

64

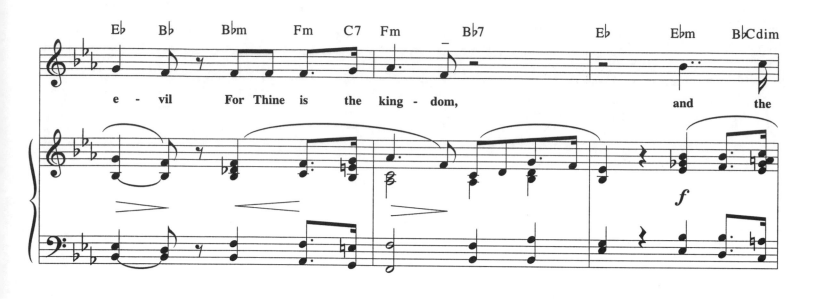

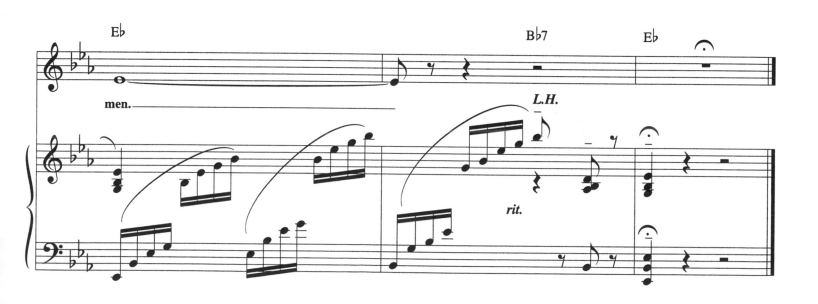

Michael, Row The Boat Ashore

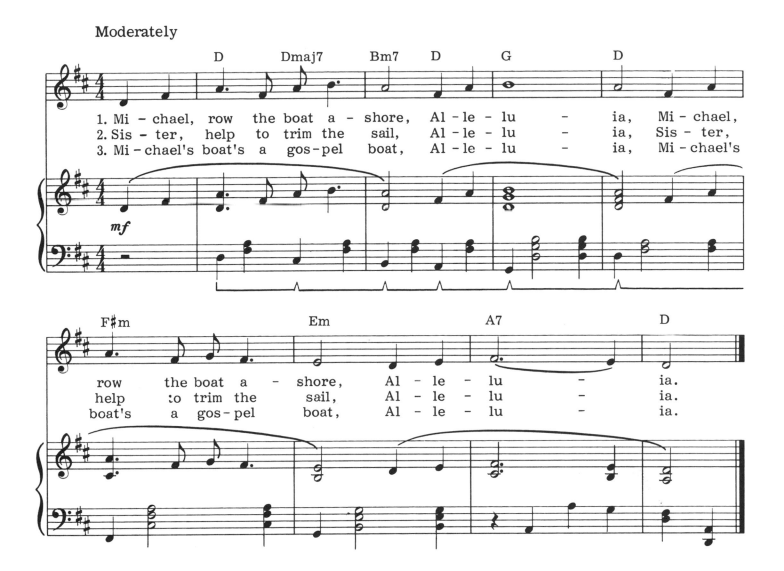

Moderately

1. Mi - chael, row the boat a - shore, Al - le - lu - ia, Mi - chael,
2. Sis - ter, help to trim the sail, Al - le - lu - ia, Sis - ter,
3. Mi - chael's boat's a gos - pel boat, Al - le - lu - ia, Mi - chael's

row the boat a - shore, Al - le - lu - ia.
help to trim the sail, Al - le - lu - ia.
boat's a gos - pel boat, Al - le - lu - ia.

4. Jordan's river is chilly and cold, Alleluia,
   Kills the body, but not the soul, Alleluia.

5. Gabriel, blow the trumpet horn, Alleluia,
   Blow the trumpet loud and long, Alleluia.

6. If you get there before I do, Alleluia,
   Tell my people I'm coming, too, Alleluia.

7. Michael, row the boat ashore, Alleluia,
   Michael, row the boat ashore, Alleluia.

Love Lifted Me

Words by James Rowe
Music by Howard E. Smith

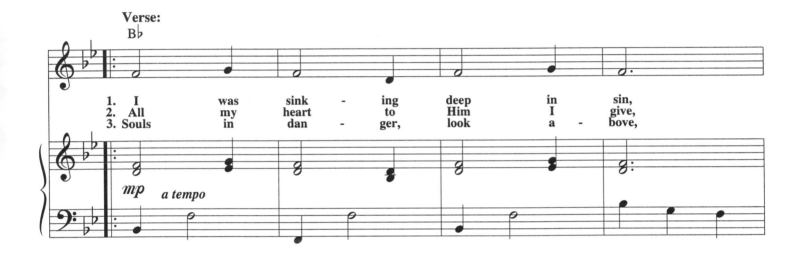

1. I was sink - ing deep in sin,
2. All my heart to Him I give,
3. Souls in dan - ger, look a - bove,

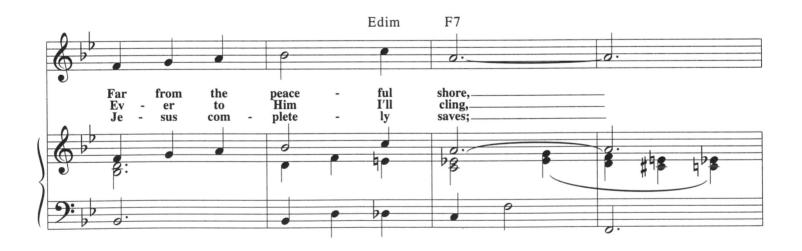

Far from the peace - ful shore,_____
Ev - er to Him I'll cling,_____
Je - sus com - plete - ly saves;_____

Nobody Knows the Trouble I've Seen

Oh Happy Day

Based on the
Doddridge-Rimbault hymn

Oh, How I Love Jesus

by Frederick Whitfield

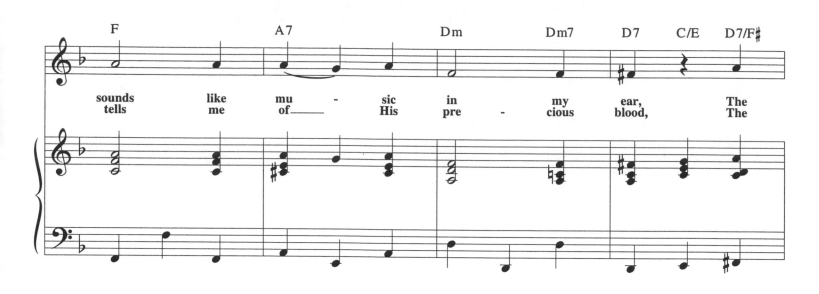

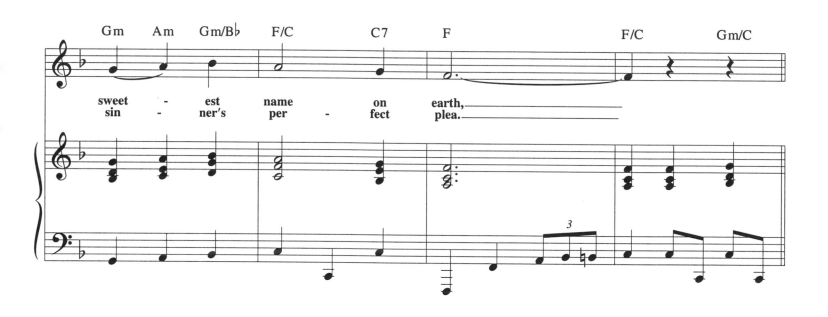

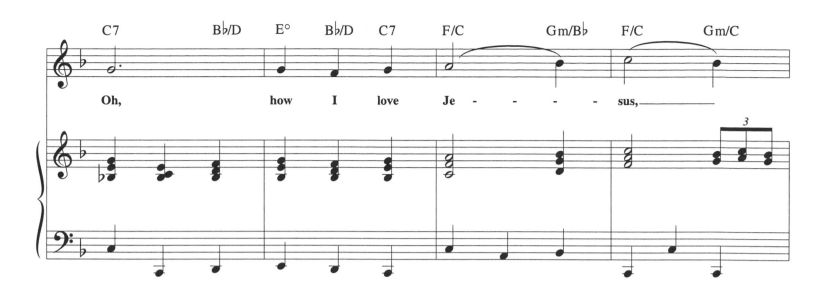

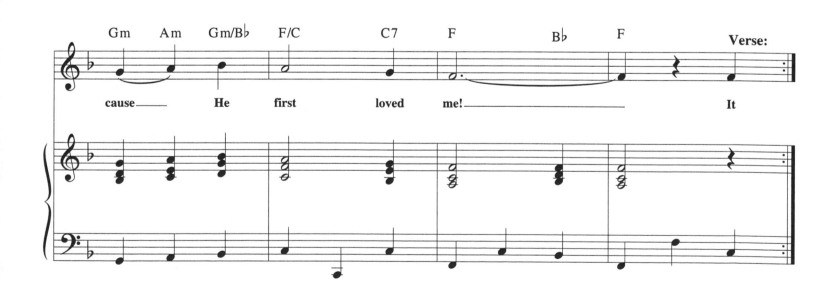

The Old Rugged Cross

Words and Music by George Bennard

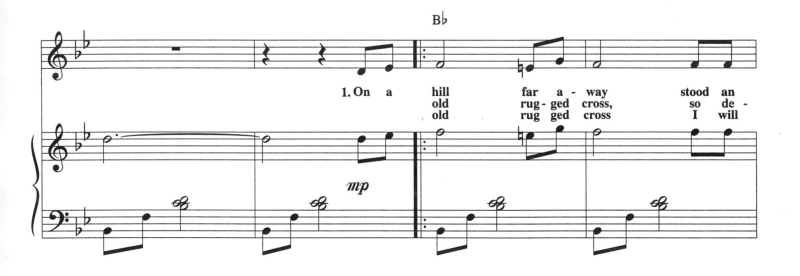

1. On a hill far a - way stood an old rug - ged cross,
old rug ged cross I will

old rug - ged cross, the em - blem of suf - f'ring and
spised by the world, has a won - drous at - trac - tion for
ev - er be true, its shame and re - proach glad - ly

81

Oh, Them Golden Slippers

Oh, my gold - en slip - pers are laid a - way, 'Cause I don't 'spect to wear them till my wed - ding day, And my long - tailed coat, that I

84

Oh, them gold-en slip-pers, Gold-en slip-pers I'm

1. goin' to wear, Be-cause they look so neat.

2. goin' to wear to walk the gold-en street.

Oh, my old banjo hangs on the wall,
'Cause it ain't been tuned since 'way last fall,
But the folks all say we'll have a good time,
When we ride up in the chariot in the morn,
There's old Brother Ben and his sister Luce,
They will telegraph the news to Uncle 'Bacco
What a great camp meeting there will be that day,
When we ride up in the chariot in the morning.

So, its goodbye children, I will have to go,
Where the rain don't fall and wind don't blow,
And your ulster coats, why, you will not need,
When you ride up in the chariot in the morn,
But your golden slippers must be nice and clean,
And your age must be just sweet sixteen,
And your white kid gloves you will have to wear,
When you ride up in the chariot in the morn.

Oh, Won't You Sit Down

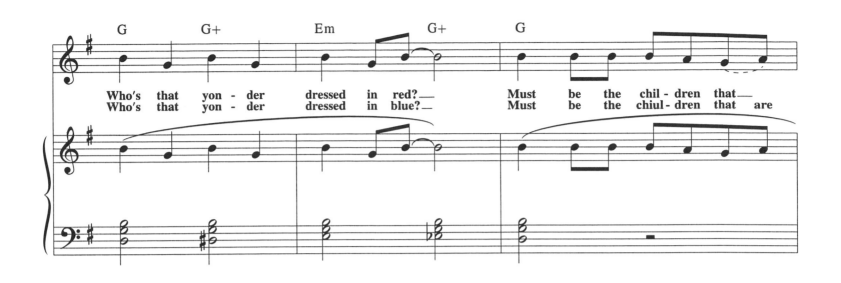

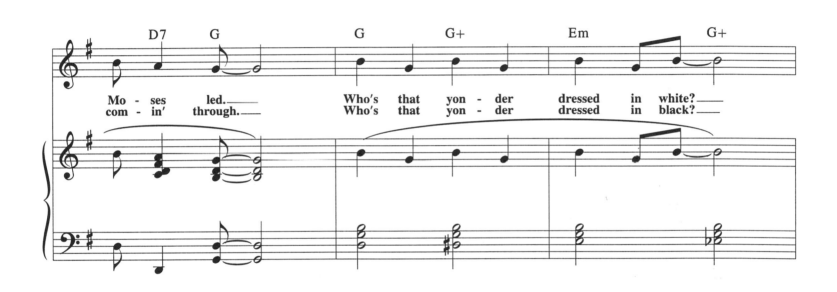

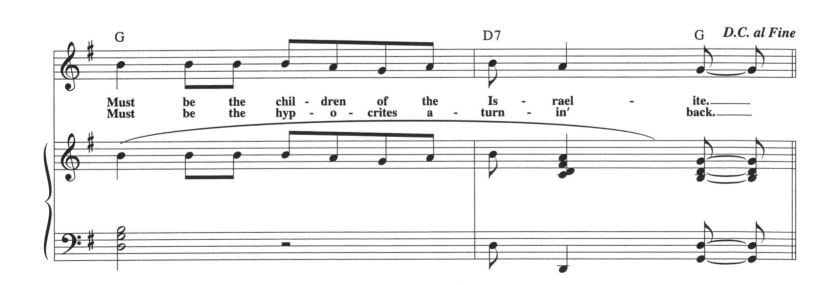

One More River To Cross

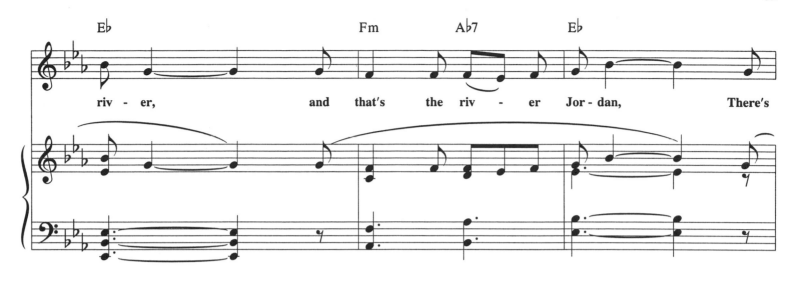

riv - er, and that's the riv - er Jor - dan, There's

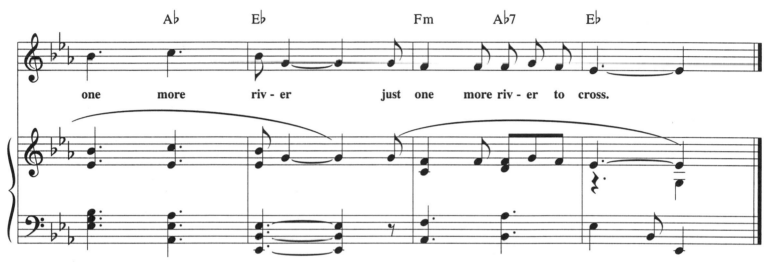

one more riv - er just one more riv - er to cross.

4. The animals went in two by two,
   There's one more river to cross,
   The rhinoceros and the kangaroo,
   Therer's one more river to cross.
   Chorus

5. The animals went in three by three,
   There's one more river to cross,
   The tall giraffe and the tiny flea,
   There's one more riovear to cross.
   Chorus

6. The animals went in four by four,
   There's one more river to cross,
   The hippopotamus stuck in the door,
   There's one more river to cross.
   Chorus

7. The animals went in five by five,
   There's one more river to cross,
   The bees took a bear for a hive,
   There's one more river to cross
   Chorus

8. The animals went in six by six,
   There's one more river to cross,
   The hyena laughed at the monkey's tricks,
   There's one more river to cross
   Chorus.

9. The animals went in seven by seven,
   There's one more river to cross,
   Said the ant to the elephant
    "Who're you shovin'?"
   There's one more river to cross.
   Chorus

10. The animals went in eight by eight,
    There's one more river to cross,
    Some were early and some were late,
    There's one more river to cross.
    Chorus

11. The animals went in nine by nine
    There's one more river to cross.
    They all formed fours and marched in line,
    There's one more river to cross.
    Chorus

12. The animals went in ten by ten,
    There's one more river to cross,
    The ark she blew her whistle then,
    There's one more river to cross.
    Chorus

13. And then the voyage did begin,
    There's one more river to cross,
    Old Noah pulled the gangplank in,
    There's one more river to cross
    Chorus.

14. They never knew where they were at,
    There's one more river to cross,
    Until the ark bumped Ararat
    There's one more river to cross.
    Chorus

Peter, Go Ring Them Bells

Precious Memories

Rock-A- My Soul

Simple Gifts

Sinner Man

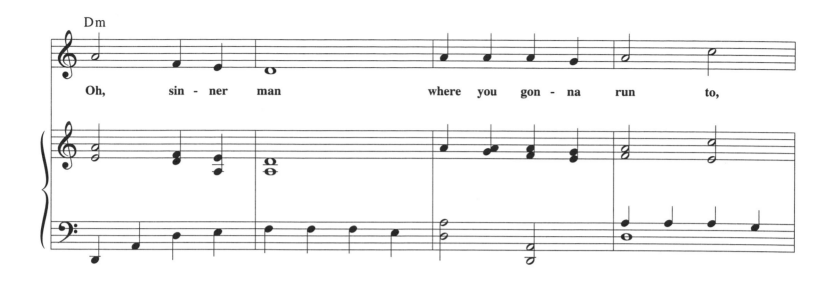

Oh, sin - ner man where you gon - na run to,

All on that day?

Run to the rock, the rock was a-melting,   (3)

Run to the sea, the sea was a-boiling,   (3)

Run to the moon, the moon was a-bleeding,   (3)

Run to the Lord, Lord won't you hide me?   (3)

Run to the Devil, Devil was a-waiting,   (3)

Oh sinner man, you oughta been a-praying   (3)

So High

Traditional

With A Strong Beat

104

This Little Light of Mine

Solid Rock

by Edward Mote

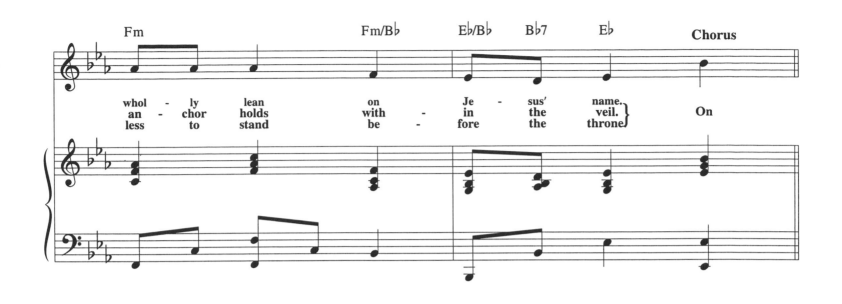

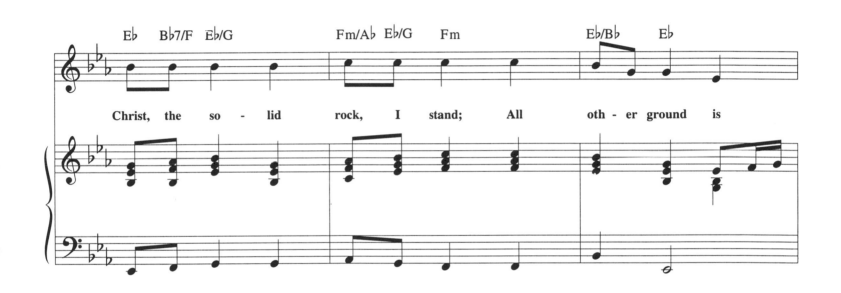

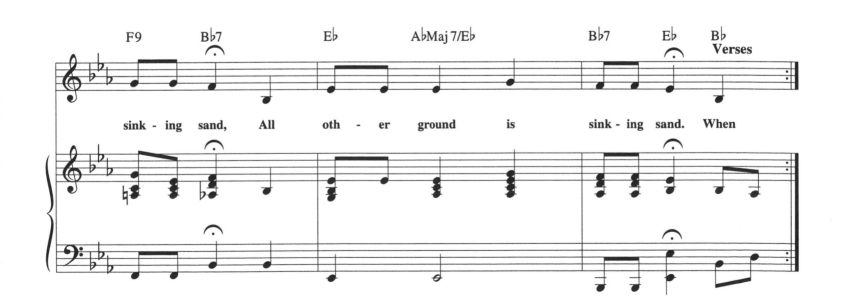

Something Within

Sometimes I Feel
Like A Motherless Child

1.Some-times I Feel Like A Moth-er-less Child, Some-times I Feel Like A
2.Some times I Feel like I'm al - most gone Some-times I feel like I'm

Moth-er-less Child Some-times I Feel Like A Moth-er-less Child, A
al - most gone, Some-times I feel like I'm al - most gone, 'Way

Standing In the Need of Prayer

Swing Low, Sweet Chariot

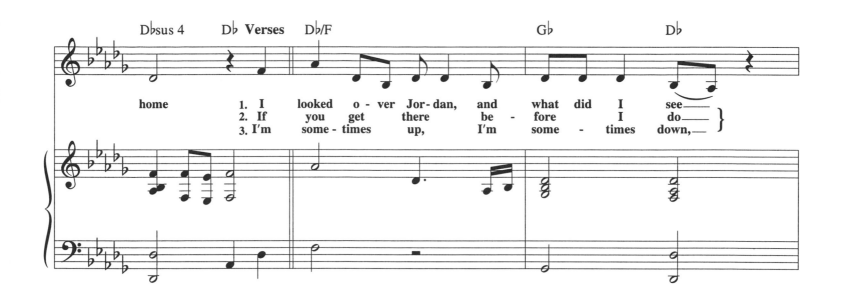

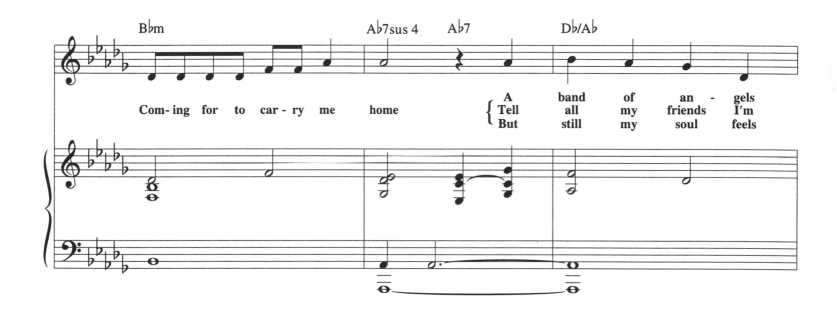

Wade in the Water

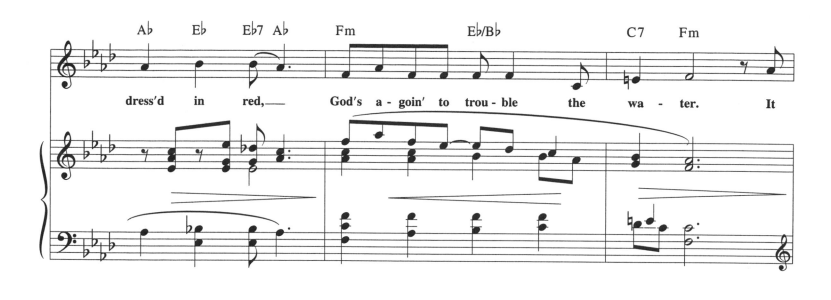

Wade in the wa - ter, chil - dren Wade in the

wa - ter, in the wa - ter, God's a - goin' to trou - ble the

wa - ter

We'll Understand It Better By and By

by Charles Albert Tindley

Were You There?

When the Saints Go Marching In

What A Friend We Have In Jesus

Up Above My Head